SOFT SIDE OF RED

Christine Shamista

SOFT SIDE OF RED

I

Sri Lanka Quietly Fades

i. Easter Sunday Bombings

I hide dazzling rabbits
under bushes
to foil our children
—still in bed.

After a late lunch
I clean the kitchen
of broken ears, legs, and heads.
My husband leans his face
to mine. I turn my head
to greet his kiss. Instead,
he whispers:
Some churches in Colombo
have been bombed.

ii. Crowned in Sunday Best

Husband reads bedtime stories.
Cross-legged, alone
on the lounge
I watch images
of ashen smoke
surrounding
white buildings
and brown bodies.

Two years ago
I was near that city,
near that church
in my Sunday best.

iii. Fair-skinned Jesus

Headline: *More than 130 Dead with Hundreds Injured.*
Death Toll to Rise.

Headline: *Multiple Bombs Blast Across the Country, Killing 290.*
Foreigners included in the death toll.
Social media blocked.
People wait to hear of loved ones.
Wait among bloodied saris, in disbelief.

Headline: *The Death Toll Rises to 321.*
The white walls, the statue of fair-skinned Jesus
in a toga style white robe flecked with red.
Missing: People. Limbs. Babies. Appahs. Ammammahs. Chellams.

Headline: *TV Celebrity Chef and Daughter First Victims.*
European fashion billionaire's three children. Other Europeans.
Two Australians. Indians. Asians.
International help, local authorities say, *is on its way.*

Headline: *359 Gone.*
Too late. Too late.
In a country weeks shy
of its ten year anniversary
of a civil war's end.

iv. So long

She fades to the back pages.
In Sydney's Inner West, I watch
my latte kulantaikal play
barefoot in the park.

II

Mantilla

Like a fragance
its touch
hovers lightly

behind the seamstress'
collection
of delicate lace

we hide

Park Road, Colombo 5, 1985

Ammappah smokes
and sips scotch
Goldie pants by his feet

upstairs
Ammammah and Mum
sort stuff
in everyday saris

out the back
in copper pots
tumeric, cumin, curry leaves
simmer

I remember

There is a Song

In quiet moments
I hear my aunties and uncles sing
fragmented hums
delivered as ash from the burning
of the Jaffna Public Library

ammahs, appammahs, ammammahs

III

Sparrow

It's not uncommon:
a sparrow
in an airport—mall—café
you've seen it—too fast to catch
and you don't want to
so you watch—and see it
tripping and hopping
and let her be

Remind Me

I forget
until students eyed me
reminding me

I forget
until I catch the odd reflection
in bus windows, reminding me

I forget
until I'm asked where I'm from
reminding me

I forget
until I see its branded beauty
my dark skin.

When You Can't Get an Uber

That's not what I mean. Where you really from?

Sri Lanka.

They used to have pretty good cricket players.
I know someone from there.
Good guy.
He's Indian too.

My Winter of Discontent

Bubble skirts. Pink and yellow fluoro.
Fingerless gloves. Leg warmers.
Side ponytails. Crimpers. Perms.
Hairspray. A match to my early burns
was the Iron Lady, who claimed
she'd replace despair with hope, doubt
with faith, discord with harmony.
But dissonant chords blared
when I was around 'Paki bashers'
and their sponges. Crew cuts
in the streets paralysed me
with fear. I longed to see that long,
grey winter, which still stains, end.

Blushes

Tall, white boys
made me wish …
but my blushes
didn't make me fairer.

Not Them. Not Me.

Age ten. Year 4. My polyester uniform sticks to my skin. First half of lunch: eat vegemite sangers in the demountable; second half: play time in the Paterson's Cursed grass. I sneeze out the past, manel in bloom, I am a leopard in Yala watching the freckled girls. I try blending in. But an overpriced white cotton rainbow-embroidered 'Sportsgirl' t-shirt, cherry blossom lip smackers, cotton candy pink nail polishes, make me darker. Not them. Not me. Each lunchtime, the sun keeps me company, and each new tan keeps me lonely. Summertime, we escape on summer holidays. We wind down, down the Clyde past Pooh Bear's corner, sucking on boiled lollies to Corrigans to gather shells, and battle bluebottle pirates on the high seas. Eat battered fish and toss chips to seagulls. Play Trivial Pursuit. Read tween fiction from Big W. Not them. Not me. My teacher couldn't teach. Her name was Harris or Tweed. Fitting. She was obsessed with England. I remember her not wanting my brown in her room and how she'd go on about Jane Austen, recreating *Pride and Prejudice* party scenes, instructing stilted dances, climbing into poses. No Jane or Lizzie, she was Mr Collins. Woden Plaza, Canberra. A hot pink fleece tracksuit, for a debut birthday party. Hot pink fleece was magical. I was indestructable. Big lawns and big houses of Arthur Circle, Forrest. I was indestructable. A room of champagne pink and blush faces, blonde and brown hair, dressed in white, khaki and denim. Not them. Not me. My child squeals. Santa has brought her fuschia fleece. *Mine, mine, mine.* She discovers hers. Claims hers. Not them. Not me.

Brown

i.

I sit in so called progressive executive meetings where I, a minority member fulfilling a diversity quota (qualified, experienced to be here, yet still second guessing), sit through a white woman who rarely smiles and seems to always get her way, rationalise allegations of racism by claiming *he's just upset he didn't get his way.* Another pipes in, *but we should listen to what we need to hear.* She's brushed over quickly, as someone else wants their five minutes, to share their anecdote. Within seconds a response is drafted, the next agenda item is addressed, and us brown people are the only ones who haven't had our say. We look at each other … knowingly …

ii.

Under the doona with my son and daughter, I close Bronwyn Bancroft's *Colours of Australia.* We speak of our favourite colours: the greens of the trees they love to climb; blues, deep and changing like the ocean they love to splash in; red and silver, the colours of his favourite superhero, Ironman. *My skin, Mummy. It's brown!* he says, smiling. *Mine too!* she says, proudly. I surprise myself that I'm surprised. I was expecting ... what I think I felt.

iii.

It's good to be fair, don't get dark, aunties told me throughout my childhood. *Stay out of the sun, stay fair.* Others can see the benefits of my darkness. I see interviewers mentally tick the second diversity box, when they see me. I see the surprise of some, when they hear me speak, in my unexpected accent. Different, but still the same.

iv.

Brown—the colour of the earth, of tree trunks, whisky, bourbon, tea, cocoa beans, autumn; composite, made when you mix red, yellow and blue; the colour that surveys say Europeans and Americans dislike most; the colour of the most overlooked, discarded, colonised, resilient. We, of the same blood, same bones, human race. Same same, but still treated so differently.

IV

Ammammah

Ammammah was from Winston's Ceylon
—not Stalin's.
I like to think of her Colombo house
—the large square marble French floor tiles.
I remember the aerogramme she sent me
—addressed from Sri Lanka.
Ammammah, tell me about your Sri Lanka
—she bounces her crossed leg, causing her sari to quiver.
At one hundred, her prefered company
—a cup of tea and a Marie biscuit: her Daily Bread.

Nineteen eighty-five. My first trip back to Sri Lanka. We stayed in Park Lane, our White House, built by Ammappah. The house, remarkably untouched in this decades long war. With the attention on my new baby sister, I wandered the white rendered concrete archways, under ceiling fans, on wooden floors, past cane chairs—like the place was mine, absorbing those with flecks and specks of me, experiencing what I would later turn to, over and over again, feeling at home in this new experience. Those hot, wet Colombo days were filled with shadowing family and watching the cook cook in her metal pots and bowls, slicing, stirring, simmering and serving out curries with her coconut-shell spoons. I drank Coke from a glass bottle and played with a new friend on the beach. Our fourteen day holiday clipped to four, *just to avoid troubles*, I was told. A phrase I'd hear often.

And so we began life in our new home, Canberra—kan-buh-ruh—a large country town disguised as the capital city: barren, brown, dry heat with no family or friends. Starting from scratch again. Some thirty years later, at a local community art exhibition in Summer Hill, I stand near my parents, reading about the Anuradhapura massacre from a sheet of bleached white A4 paper. And then read about what came before this massacre in Mulliyavalai, Vaddakkandal, Puthukkudiyiruppu, Trincomalee, Valvettiturai, from two sheets of bleached white A4 paper. And then read about what came after this massacre in Kumudini, Thambiluvil, Killiveddy from another sheet of bleached white A4 paper.

Appammah's House

Two days gone—the house is untouched.
The speckled black stone-topped
kitchen bench that sits on the baby blue cabinetry
holds the familiar benchtop gathering:
jar of Nescafé Blend 43
box of Dilmah Extra Strength teabags
mixture of metal and plastic teaspoons
and mismatched mugs upside down
on the faded blue plastic draining board
complimented by the faded red tin of spicy murrukhu.
Behind my reflection on the nineteen-seventies
display cabinet in the lounge room
are the floral ceramic plates, cups & saucers
and family photos—black & white and coloured.
Appammah's pills are still on the mantle.
A single white hair hangs
caught on the cream crochet covering
of Appammah's armchair;
its descent matches my slow-sinking tea leaves.

Swimming

I know where home is,
because when it shakes,
light disappears, my breaths
become shallow, and
I have to swim hard
to find which way is up.

TO NUWARA ELIYA

I empty my mints
on the back seat
and twirl my
curly black hair
trapped in a pony-tail
as our minibus winds
its way along
to Nuwara Eliya.

V

Vīṭu

i.

My youth was lost in Sherwood Forest.

ii.

She wakes me with Her sound
of Colombo streets and family names.
I feel Her skin, as I brush against Her.
I take in Her jewellery of mosques,
cathedrals, and temples; mangoes,
pineapples, jackfruit; bread carts;
electric rickshaws—green, blue, and red;
a monk wrapped in a marigold orange robe.
Her hair combed and curled
by the sultry air of coastline towns,
paddy fields, dark stumped rubber
and towering, bendy coconut trees,
and red bottlebrush-like rambutans.
I walk behind Her—Her who is Mum,
aunty, cousin and niece—along
a skinny footpath which winds
around her waist where
sarees and sarongs fly in Her breeze.
She leads me up a grassy hill
which looks over the coastline.
I squint my eyes toward my other home.
Behind here, is She, my first.

Her perfume of palms,
giant bamboo and orchids.
I know here.
Her tears rise and crash.
Her tears can be deadly.
A Peraliya sign reminds me:
The original organiser
of this turtle farm was my father …
After he died my sister … took over
this place. She died in the tsunami
of 2004 along with the destruction
of the turtle farm.

She is a young, dark-skinned, slim man
wearing a shirt that matches the sky,
flashing a smile as he stands under
the 'New Ranweli Spice Garden' sign.
He calls out to us in English:
Come, come. Welcome.
I look up from Her uneven ground.
She is the garden,
a billion shades of green;
Her saree, a vast field
of Tamil women
plucking tea leaves.
I walk on Her ground. Her toes burst
out of the cinnamon coloured dirt.
Her body, a garden of spice and oil.
I hold a sprig of red and green pepper,
Her green arms crawl over and around
a small cream rendered house
with a sloping roof. She invites me in.
Under Her shade, we recline.

Through wooden plantation shutters,
I hear Her hum, and smell Her spicy,
sweet breath of nutmeg, fenugreek,
ginger, cinnamon, cocoa.
I lie back lazily on a bench, rubbing
curry leaves, releasing the smells
from kitchens of Ammammah,
Appammah, aunties, Mum.

At dusk, I laze down Her belly
to Sri Dalada Maligawa,
the home of Buddha's tooth.
We watch a gentle, constant stream of people enter
the Temple of the Sacred Tooth Relic.
Candles shine brighter
as the sunlight disappears,
the pastel pinks and oranges
darken and disappear.

My final afternoon with Her.
We have high tea at The Verandah
at Galle Face Hotel
facing the Indian Ocean.
We witness two weddings,
Kandyan dancing, bagpipes and singing.

I walk on Her green carpet,
merging with others.
I call out to a small boy
as I kick back his soccer ball.
His parents come to me,
matching my accent with theirs.
They too, are from Sydney's Inner West.
I am pulled away from Her, back.

iii.

Outside the airport
a seaport is being built
funded by a foreign 'ally'
helping to expand
Sri Lanka to the world.

Inside the airport
I'm in the duty-free shop
buying Lego for
my four-year-old son.

iv.

I return. Land.
Like my ancestral home,
this is a land
full of troubling history.

v.

Lockdown, six months in, I flick through various Sri Lankan cookbooks. Appammah would prepare her dishes from scratch, grinding with her mortar and pestle. I tried learning to cook from Mum:

I coat the drumsticks.

In what?

Just a bit of the curry powder …

How much?

and garlic and …

And?

and I leave it for a bit.

How long?

Mum?

I don't remember what Appammah did, or or how she did it. But I remember:

How is school?

What's your favourite subject?

What do you want to do when you grow up?

You remember Aunty Raji? Her granddaughter is your age, wants to study medicine. You don't need to. Your parents are doctors. We don't need more. You could marry one!

VI

Softened

She wept. Because
a lifetime of grief
—in many forms—
softened her

Periwinkle Blue

is today's sky, no cotton
wool-like clouds
I feel the sun sit gently
on my skin, gently easing
me into this moment
and I surrender to it, dance
with it, not wanting to taint
it with my plans and agenda
where any brash move
could erase the simplicity
of what surrounds me, and now
I think of you, who
always accompanies me in these
moments; and so we recline
into this day, letting it be
our afternoon hammock.

Spoken

A woman
in tight jeans,
a hot pink midriff
and black Docs
wearing all
she carries
bold and proud

soft spoken loud

Piercings

Be careful of that woman.
Though she's quiet,
on the other side of forty,
she gives less fucks.

Punctuated by violent shades of red—I piece together constellations in softer shades: Mum's roses, my baby pink fifth Minnie Mouse birthday cake, biscuit crumbs on Ammammah's coral cardigan, sepia photos of my Sri Lankan childhood, champagne vinegar string hoppers with Mum's dynamite chicken curry, the peach bubble skirt Ammappah bought me, snacking on ripe mandarins and persimmons in Cabramatta's street markets, stealing a lick of my husband's Turkish Delight ice cream, blaze orange Aperol spritzes, fushia toenails, the perfumed Pink Palace lilies on Appammah's coffin wreath, the Phalaenopsis orchids I bought for myself, the flowers in my mother-in-law's terracotta pots, slicing Pink Lady apples for lunchboxes, velvety amaranth peonies, our flamingo quilt, cherries at Christmas.

Chord

One by one the notes are released

Then, as they blur into each other,
there's a moment of dissonance

until

they all fit together
making it easy
to forget that once, all this
did not exist as

one

and just as you sit in this perfect
chord, it moves away and another
begins to form, and you

watch

the harpist's fingers caress strings
simple movements with transcendent

sounds

like a sunset whose beauty cannot be
frozen in time but moves, life
not even just this once, will it

pause

and you sigh and breathe

Soft Side of Red
by Christine Shamista

for Appammah, Ammammah, and Mum & Dad

The author acknowledges this collection was written on the lands of the Aboriginal and Torres Strait Islander peoples, and pays respect to their elders, past and present.

Thanks to the *HB Higgins Scholarship for Poetry—University of Melbourne.*

Acknowledgement is made for poems previously published: *Conversations* (Pandanus Books, ANU: Canberra, 2002); *Contemporary Asian Australian Poets* (Puncher and Wattmann, Glebe NSW, 2013); *FourW* (Wagga Wagga NSW, 2014); *'A Sweatshop in a Red Room'* (Red Room Poetry, Australia, 2019); *Sweatshop Women: Volume 1* and *2* (Sweatshop Western Sydney Literacy Movement Inc., Parramatta NSW, 2019/2020); *Racism: Stories on fear, hate & bigotry* (Sweatshop Western Sydney Literacy Movement Inc., Parramatta NSW, 2021); *Resilience* (Ultimo Press, Ultimo NSW, 2022).

First published 2023

POETRY

ISBN: 978-0-6456337-7-1

BOOK, TYPSETTING, AND LOGO DESIGN
Mountains Brown Press

PUBLISHER
Life Before Man

Gazebo Books
PO Box 375
Summer Hill
New South Wales 2130
Australia

gazebobooks.com.au/life-before-man/

2 4 6 8 10 9 7 5 3 1

This book was made possible thanks to Anthony Mark Day